# SOME MAJOR EVENTS IN WORLD WAR II

## THE EUROPEAN THEATER

**1939** SEPTEMBER—Germany invades Poland; Great Britain, France, Australia, & New Zealand declare war on Germany; Battle of the Atlantic begins. NOVEMBER—Russia invades Finland.

**1940** APRIL—Germany invades Denmark & Norway. MAY—Germany invades Belgium, Luxembourg, & The Netherlands; British forces retreat to Dunkirk and escape to England. JUNE—Italy declares war on Britain & France; France surrenders to Germany. JULY—Battle of Britain begins. SEPTEMBER—Italy invades Egypt; Germany, Italy, & Japan form the Axis countries. OCTOBER—Italy invades Greece. NOVEMBER—Battle of Britain over. DECEMBER—Britain attacks Italy in North Africa.

**1941** JANUARY—Allies take Tobruk. FEBRUARY—Rommel arrives at Tripoli. APRIL—Germany invades Greece & Yugoslavia. JUNE—Allies are in Syria; Germany invades Russia. JULY—Russia joins Allies. AUGUST—Germans capture Kiev. OCTOBER—Germany reaches Moscow. DECEMBER—Germans retreat from Moscow; Japan attacks Pearl Harbor; United States enters war against Axis nations.

**1942** MAY—first British bomber attack on Cologne. JUNE—Germans take Tobruk. SEPTEMBER—Battle of Stalingrad begins. OCTOBER—Battle of El Alamein begins. NOVEMBER—Allies recapture Tobruk; Russians counterattack at Stalingrad.

**1943** JANUARY—Allies take Tripoli. FEBRUARY—German troops at Stalingrad surrender. APRIL—revolt of Warsaw Ghetto Jews begins. MAY—German and Italian resistance in North Africa is over; their troops surrender in Tunisia; Warsaw Ghetto revolt is put down by Germany. JULY—allies invade Sicily; Mussolini put in prison. SEPTEMBER—Allies land in Italy; Italians surrender; Germans occupy Rome; Mussolini rescued by Germany. OCTOBER—Allies capture Naples; Italy declares war on Germany. NOVEMBER—Russians recapture Kiev.

**1944** JANUARY—Allies land at Anzio. JUNE—Rome falls to Allies; Allies land in Normandy (D-Day). JULY—assassination attempt on Hitler fails. AUGUST—Allies land in southern France. SEPTEMBER—Brussels freed. OCTOBER—Athens liberated. DECEMBER—Battle of the Bulge.

**1945** JANUARY—Russians free Warsaw. FEBRUARY—Dresden bombed. APRIL—Americans take Belsen and Buchenwald concentration camps; Russians free Vienna; Russians take over Berlin; Mussolini killed; Hitler commits suicide. MAY—Germany surrenders; Goering captured.

## THE PACIFIC THEATER

**1940** SEPTEMBER—Japan joins Axis nations Germany & Italy.

**1941** APRIL—Russia & Japan sign neutrality pact. DECEMBER—Japanese launch attacks against Pearl Harbor, Hong Kong, the Philippines, & Malaya; United States and Allied nations declare war on Japan; China declares war on Japan, Germany, & Italy; Japan takes over Guam, Wake Island, & Hong Kong; Japan attacks Burma.

**1942** JANUARY—Japan takes over Manila; Japan invades Dutch East Indies. FEBRUARY—Japan takes over Singapore; Battle of the Java Sea. APRIL—Japanese overrun Bataan. MAY—Japan takes Mandalay; Allied forces in Philippines surrender to Japan; Japan takes Corregidor; Battle of the Coral Sea. JUNE—Battle of Midway; Japan occupies Aleutian Islands. AUGUST—United States invades Guadalcanal in the Solomon Islands.

**1943** FEBRUARY—Guadalcanal taken by U.S. Marines. MARCH—Japanese begin to retreat in China. APRIL—Yamamoto shot down by U.S. Air Force. MAY—U.S. troops take Aleutian Islands back from Japan. JUNE—Allied troops land in New Guinea. NOVEMBER—U.S. Marines invade Bougainville & Tarawa.

**1944** FEBRUARY—Truk liberated. JUNE—Saipan attacked by United States. JULY—battle for Guam begins. OCTOBER—U.S. troops invade Philippines; Battle of Leyte Gulf won by Allies.

**1945** JANUARY—Luzon taken; Burma Road won back. MARCH—Iwo Jima freed. APRIL—Okinawa attacked by U.S. troops; President Franklin Roosevelt dies; Harry S. Truman becomes president. JUNE—United States takes Okinawa. AUGUST—atomic bomb dropped on Hiroshima; Russia declares war on Japan; atomic bomb dropped on Nagasaki. SEPTEMBER—Japan surrenders.

# WORLD AT WAR
# The Home Front

# WORLD AT WAR

# The Home Front

By R. Conrad Stein

Consultant:
Professor Robert L. Messer, Ph.D.
Department of History
University of Illinois, Chicago

CHILDRENS PRESS ®

CHICAGO

On December 8, 1941, the day after Pearl Harbor was attacked, American President
Franklin Delano Roosevelt signed the declaration of war against Japan.

FRONTISPIECE:
Theater usherettes lead a parade during a 1942 war bond rally in Philadelphia.

**Library of Congress Cataloging-in-Publication Data**

Stein, R. Conrad.
  The home front.

  (World at war)
  Includes index.
  Summary: Describes life on the "home front"
during World War II, when children collected
newspapers, movies were filled with propaganda,
working women became commonplace, and
necessities were rationed.
  1.   United States—History—1933-1945—
Juvenile literature.   2.   World War, 1939-1945—
Juvenile literature.   [1.   United States—
History—1933-1945.   2.   World War, 1939-
1945—United States]   I.   Title.   II.   Series.
E806.S783   1986         940.53'73         86-11730
ISBN 0-516-04769-8

PICTURE CREDITS:
WIDE WORLD: Cover, pages 9, 15, 23, 25 (bottom
right), 27, 31, 33 (bottom), 36 (top), 39
UPI: Pages 4, 6, 8, 10, 11, 12, 19, 22, 25 (top, bottom
left), 33 (top right), 36 (bottom right), 41, 44, 45,
46
HISTORICAL PICTURES SERVICE, CHICAGO: Pages 13,
30, 36 (bottom left), 37, 42, 43
PHOTRI: Pages 14, 17 (top), 18, 20, 28, 35
NATIONAL ARCHIVES: Pages 17 (bottom), 24, 33
(top left), 34

COVER PHOTO:
During the war, scrap metal was collected to be
converted into armaments. These New York City
youngsters were cutting, washing, and flattening
old cans to ready them for recycling.

PROJECT EDITOR:
Joan Downing

CREATIVE DIRECTOR:
Margrit Fiddle

The routine Sunday afternoon was shattered by anxious words: "Hey, Dad, come here and listen to the radio!" or "Mom, where's Pearl Harbor?" As radio reports grew more urgent, people were gripped by mixed emotions—disbelief, shock, outrage, horror. All Americans old enough to remember December 7, 1941, can recall precisely where they were and what they were doing when the stunning news came that Japanese planes had bombed the United States naval base in Hawaii, thereby plunging the nation into war.

Suddenly, air-raid drills were being conducted in deadly earnest. At night, sirens blared and volunteer air-raid wardens patrolled the streets during practice blackouts. Any household careless enough to leave a light burning behind uncovered windows was given a warning. None of the United States' enemies had airplanes with enough range to fly from their home bases to America's shores. Nevertheless, cities as far inland as St. Louis practiced air-raid drills.

Everyone wanted to do their part in the war effort. These volunteer air-raid workers were waiting in line to receive protective helmets.

The air-raid scares prompted the immediate mobilization of the American people. Everyone pitched in to contribute in some way to the war effort. American civilians during World War II lived in a turbulent world of patriotism, sacrifice, hope, and tears. Journalists called this world the home front.

Home-front Americans tried to prepare for the possibility of enemy attack. During air-raid drills, students ducked under their desks (above left) and people on the street took refuge wherever they could (above right). Using a dummy, a civilian defense rescue squad (below) demonstrated how to remove a bombing-attack victim from the rubble of a damaged building.

Volunteers in Seattle follow a United States Navy recruiting truck a few days after the attack on Pearl Harbor.

In the weeks following the attack on Pearl Harbor, army and navy recruiting stations were flooded with volunteers. A new tune on the jukeboxes blared out:

> Good-bye, Mama
> I'm off to Yokohama
> For the red, white, and blue,
> My country and you.

In small towns, high-school bands played and American Legion veterans hoisted the flag as local boys were marched off to training camp.

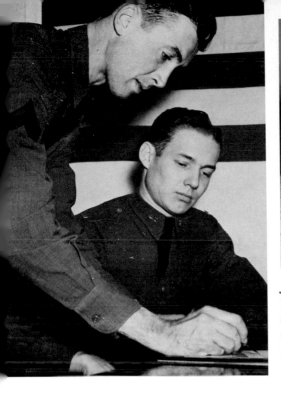

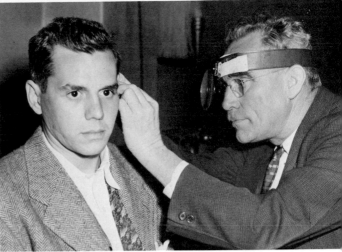

Jimmy Stewart (left) and Desi Arnaz (right, undergoing army medical check-up) were among the many celebrities who set an example for other Americans by signing up for the armed services.

In New York City, nineteen-year-old Stanley Rosmarin quit college to enlist in the army. His eleven-year-old brother Rick boasted to everyone on the block, "My big brother's going to be a soldier." After Stanley left for basic training, young Rick fell asleep each night looking at his brother's bar-mitzvah picture, which hung in the bedroom they had shared. In the front-door window, his parents proudly displayed a white banner with a single blue star. The banner had been provided by the War Department to announce to neighbors and passersby that the household had a son or daughter in the armed forces.

Americans showed their patriotism in many ways. After winning a contest looking for the "typical American family," the Jones family (above) turned its thousand-dollar prize into defense bonds. The five boys of the Sullivan family (below) enlisted in the navy together after hearing that one of their friends had been killed at Pearl Harbor. In November 1942, all five brothers died when their ship was sunk during a battle near Guadalcanal.

In 1944, the United States government presented five Purple Hearts to Mr. and Mrs. Thomas Sullivan, the parents of the Sullivan boys.

A banner with five stars hung outside the Sullivan house in Waterloo, Iowa. The five Sullivan boys had joined the navy together after hearing that a childhood friend of theirs had been killed during the attack on Pearl Harbor. The brothers insisted that they remain together, and the navy reluctantly agreed to station them on the same ship. On November 14, 1942, their ship was sunk off Guadalcanal. All five Sullivan boys died. Not since the Civil War had a single family lost so many members in wartime service. Soon after the tragedy, a film about the brothers called *The Fighting Sullivans* was made. The navy even named a destroyer in their honor — U.S.S. *The Sullivans.* Throughout the war, the bereaved parents of the Sullivan boys were hailed as heroes of the home front.

Fearing that the home front might become infiltrated by enemy agents, the American government printed posters warning people not to give away any information that could be of value to the enemy.

The home front had supposed villains as well as heroes. In 1942, rumors abounded that spies and saboteurs with plans to blow up bridges, defense plants, and ship canals had landed in America from submarines. In reality, the Germans made only a few feeble attempts to land saboteurs, and the Japanese made none at all. Still, some alarmist newspapers and radio commentators warned that secret agents were lurking around every corner. People in small towns viewed newcomers suspiciously, especially if a stranger had a trace of a European accent. In coastal areas, groups of boys patrolled the beaches hoping to become heroes by capturing invaders.

On the West Coast, invasion hysteria took its ugliest form. After Pearl Harbor, white Americans

On the West Coast, volunteer civil-defense workers patrolled areas that were likely to be targets of sabotage, such as the Golden Gate Bridge in San Francisco.

in California, Oregon, and Washington suddenly began suspecting their Japanese American neighbors of being cunning enemy agents. Rumors spread that Japanese Americans had been seen operating secret radio stations and signaling Japanese submarines at night with flashlights. Though there was not a shred of proof that Japanese Americans were in any way disloyal, panicky whites demanded that they be moved away from the shores.

In the *San Francisco Examiner*, reporter Henry McLemore wrote, "Why treat Japs well here? I am for the immediate removal of every Japanese."

In February of 1942, President Franklin D. Roosevelt signed Executive Order 9066. Under its provisions, 112,000 Japanese Americans were forced out of their homes and sent to "relocation camps" in desolate areas miles away from the West Coast. Two thirds of the detainees had been born in the United States. Their rights as American citizens were completely disregarded. The relocation centers were ugly, barbed-wire-enclosed barracks patrolled by guards armed with automatic rifles. Even President Roosevelt once referred to the centers as "concentration camps."

Most Japanese Americans lost the homes and businesses they had built up slowly for a generation or more. A young girl named Yuriko Hohiri remembered the raid made on her home just before her family was marched off to the camps: "The war became real for me when two FBI agents came to our home in Long Beach. It was a few months after December 7 [Pearl Harbor Day]. I was twelve. . . . One man went right into the kitchen. As I watched, he looked under the sink and he looked into the oven."

Left: Carrying only a few belongings, a Japanese American family awaits evacuation to one of the barbed-wire-enclosed relocation camps. Below: Before being evacuated, a Japanese American woman stands in front of the stately Los Angeles home she was forced to abandon. Japanese Americans who returned home after being released from the camps often found that their homes and businesses had been sold or vandalized.

The relocation camps were set up in desolate areas miles away from the coast. At the camp in Manzanar, California (above), families were forced to live in drab, one-room "apartments" in flimsy wooden barracks covered with tar paper.

Japanese Americans were kept at the camps for about three years before being allowed to rejoin American society. While incarcerated, many of them assembled each morning to raise the American flag, pledge allegiance, and stand at attention while the camp drum-and-bugle corps played "The Star-Spangled Banner." Even more astonishing, hundreds of the young men living in the barbed-wire prisons signed up for the army. Most Japanese American soldiers were members of the 100/442 Regimental Combat Team. That unit won more medals for bravery than any other American outfit in World War II.

By 1943, the American labor force was producing war materials in amazing quantities. Some two hundred thousand companies converted their operations from civilian to war production. This photograph shows production of B-29 bomber wings at a New Jersey aircraft plant.

By 1943, the American home front was producing war materials in staggering quantities. A factory in Detroit, Michigan was turning out a thousand tanks a month. A nearby plant was able to produce one giant B-24 bomber every sixty-three minutes. On the West Coast, freight-hauling "Liberty" ships were assembled in just twenty-four working days. World War II was to a great extent an arms-production race between the Allied and Axis powers. The clear winner of that race was the United States. American workers manufactured more war materials than did the rest of the world combined.

American workers responded enthusiastically to the government's appeal for an all-out commitment to war production. American production hit an all-time peak, and unemployment virtually disappeared. By the end of the war, the United States had churned out 296,429 airplanes, 86,333 tanks, and 11,900 ships.

When Pearl Harbor was attacked, the United States was just beginning to recover from the Great Depression of the 1930s. During the most bitter years of the depression, one of every four workers had been unemployed. But after the war began, factories were begging for workers. Wartime prosperity, however, was a mixed blessing. A story was told about a woman who, while traveling on a bus, said loudly, "Well, my husband is making more money than ever before, so I hope this war lasts a good long while." Another woman passenger rose, slapped her, and with tears rolling down her cheeks blurted out, "That's for my boy who's in the marines. I worry about him every day."

Life on the home front was full of conflicting emotions. Happiness over full employment and high earnings was mixed with anxiety about those in the service. The families that had blue stars in their windows lived in constant fear of an unexpected knock on the door. That could mean a messenger with a cold and impersonal telegram: "THE WAR DEPARTMENT REGRETS TO INFORM YOU YOUR SON WAS KILLED. . . . " After such a telegram was received, the blue star in the window was replaced with a gold star. Young Rick Rosmarin knew of gold-star households. Before he went to bed each night, Rick glanced at his brother's bar-mitzvah picture and prayed that he would come home safely.

Home-front Americans helped pay for the enormous cost of the war by buying War Bonds, which could be purchased in denominations ranging from twenty-five dollars to ten thousand dollars. This huge cash register was built in the middle of Times Square to record total sales of war bonds in New York during the nation's fifth war-loan drive in 1944.

These youngsters were crowned "King and Queen of Scrapland" for collecting an entire ton of scrap metal during a New York City scrap drive.

The war effort so engulfed the home front that even children were swept up in its frenzy. Youngsters in cities and towns collected scrap metal to be converted into bombs and shells. Posters announced, "The iron in one old shovel can make four hand grenades." Small armies of children scrounged the alleys looking for discarded pots, pans, tin cans, and bedsprings. The words of a Bing Crosby song drummed the message:

> Junk ain't junk no more
> 'Cause junk can win the war.

Two children participating in a scrap-paper drive add their contributions to a pile of old newspapers. Scrap paper was recycled and then used to package armaments.

Children also collected wastepaper, which was made into the cartridge belts used to carry ammunition. In Chicago schools, every Wednesday was declared "Paper Day," and students hauled tied-up bundles of newspapers to school. The teacher measured the bundles with a ruler to determine which was the biggest. The student who brought in the thickest pile of newspapers was awarded a gold pin that could be worn proudly for the rest of the week. In five-months' time, Chicago schoolchildren collected eighteen thousand tons of newspapers.

Taking part in home-front activities gave children a real sense of involvement in the war. These two children (left) were helping to kick off a war-bond drive in their hometown of Alexandria, New York. A group of Chicago boys (below left) earned money to be spent on war bonds by selling fruit and vegetable containers that they made out of old, broken crates. Five-year-old Anthony Marino (below right) combed the streets of his New York City neighborhood noisily asking his neighbors to donate scrap metal.

Comic-book heroes stopped fighting criminals and turned their attention to battling the Germans and the Japanese. Superman fought spies and saboteurs. Amazingly, however, he failed his army physical. His X-ray vision melted the machine used to check the recruits' eyes! Red-cloaked Captain Marvel matched wits with the evil genius Dr. Savannah, who worked for shadowy German agents. One of the sinister doctor's inventions was an intelligent worm named Mr. Mind. When finally captured by Captain Marvel, the worm hissed, "Curses, you big red cheese."

Boys became amateur experts on the weapons rolling out of the factories. They argued over which was the better vehicle — the Grant tank or the Sherman tank. At a glance, most boys could distinguish a Mustang fighter plane from a Thunderbolt or a B-17 bomber from a B-24. In empty lots, boys sat in make-believe foxholes and shot at enemies with imaginary machine guns. Blocks of wood floating in back-alley puddles became blazing battleships.

Americans were urged to grow their own fruits and vegetables in backyard "Victory gardens" so that more food would be available for those fighting overseas. The 20.5 million Victory gardens planted in 1943 accounted for one-third of all the vegetables eaten in the United States that year.

There was no television at the time, but radio programs aimed at young listeners spun wartime adventure yarns. The daily show "Terry and the Pirates" told of a squadron of fighter planes stationed in the Pacific. It seemed that every week at least one of the squadron's members was shot out of the sky, prompting a heroic rescue. At the movies, cartoon characters urged one and all to do their part in the war effort. Donald Duck, Mickey Mouse, Bugs Bunny, and others were shown participating in scrap drives or planting small vegetable patches called Victory gardens.

As this movie poster demonstrates, most American wartime films portrayed the American soldier as a model of courage and heroism.

Most American wartime movies were filled with propaganda. Germans were depicted as heartless, obedient robots. In *Tomorrow, the World*, an orphaned German boy was pictured as the brainwashed product of Nazi society. In *The Purple Heart*, Japanese officers were portrayed as evil monsters who delighted in torturing captured American pilots. The Americans in that film, on the other hand, were models of courage. In one scene, an American pilot, though facing execution, shouted to his Japanese captors, "This is your war—you wanted it—you asked for it. And you're going to get it—and it won't be finished until your dirty little empire is wiped off the face of the earth!" A few films, however, did attempt to show the true horror of war. One was the 1945 *Story of GI Joe*, which dramatized the work of popular war correspondent Ernie Pyle. Another 1945 film, *A Walk in the Sun*, portrayed the strain of war on an American infantry platoon.

For a great number of Americans, life on the home front meant long, dreary hours working in war plants. A sixty-hour week was common for war-industry workers. Often, factories ran on swing shifts—three eight-hour relays that kept the machines in constant motion around the clock. A factory building buzzing with activity in the middle of the night was a hallmark of the home front.

These mail carriers were among the millions of women who responded to the shortage of manpower during the war by taking on jobs that had traditionally been held only by men.

Nothing in American life changed more than the role of women. Before the 1940s, women were thought of first as mothers and homemakers. Working women were usually teachers, librarians, salesclerks, or secretaries. But as the war sent more and more men overseas, women began to take on jobs previously held only by men. Suddenly, women had to become gas-station attendants, mail carriers, cab drivers, soda jerks, and elevator operators.

Working women made their most profound impact in the factories. Early in the war, factory managers were reluctant to hire women because

Women employees at a California aircraft plant polish the noses of Douglas A-20 attack bombers.

they believed women had no understanding of machinery. But as the war dragged on and the shortage of manpower became more critical, factories began recruiting women workers. "If you can make a cake, then you can put powder in a shell casing," read an ad posted by one munitions plant. In West-Coast aircraft factories, a fictional character named Rosie the Riveter became a popular figure. Posters showed her attractively clad in overalls, holding a riveting machine, and urging her fellow workers to report to the plant every day. By late 1944, women made up 40 percent of the work force in aircraft-assembly plants and 12 percent in shipyards.

Although women workers made an enormous contribution to the war effort, they earned an estimated 40 percent less than men. Supervisory positions continued to be reserved for men. Some plants arbitrarily declared that women worked at "light assembly" and men "heavy assembly" when, in fact, both sexes did the same job. Still, the men classified as heavy-assembly workers were paid higher wages.

"Don't you know there's a war on?" This was the response given to anyone who complained about the frustrating shortage of goods during the war. Although workers were earning more money than ever before, they were able to buy precious little. A new car was out of the question, because Detroit stopped making civilian models in 1942 in order to concentrate on producing jeeps and army trucks. If a family's refrigerator, stove, toaster, iron, or alarm clock broke down, it could not be replaced. Factories during the war years produced guns, not appliances.

Skeptical employers discovered that women were just as competent as men at being welders (above left), machine operators (above right), and aircraft-assembly workers (below).

A woman buying canned goods waits for the cashier to tear off the proper number of ration stamps. The amount of stamps required for a particular item changed, sometimes weekly, as the supply of the item changed.

Everyday necessities were carefully rationed. Books of ration stamps were issued to be used when buying such scarce items as meat, fish, sugar, coffee, dairy products, and canned goods. Each rationed item was worth a certain number of stamps. To make a purchase, a shopper had to present both cash and the proper number of stamps. The rationing system allowed each American about two pounds of meat per week.

Leather was scarce, so civilians were allowed to buy no more than two pairs of shoes a year.

This photograph shows examples of food-ration stamps (left) and gas-ration cards (right).

Because Japan had seized most of the world's supply of rubber, worn-out car tires were almost impossible to replace. Gasoline rationing was imposed not only to save gas, but to conserve precious rubber. Each motorist received a windshield sticker with a letter on it ranging from *A* to *E*. An *A* sticker permitted the purchase of only three gallons of gas a week, and was issued to those who used their cars for pleasure-driving only. An *E* sticker allowed a driver unlimited gasoline, but was given only to those who could prove that driving was essential to their line of work. Policemen, clergymen, and doctors who made house calls were among the few car-owners given *E* stickers.

Rubber, needed for war materials,
became scarce after Japan seized most of
the world's supply. When President
Roosevelt called for a nationwide scrap-
rubber drive, Boy Scouts in a Wisconsin
town responded by collecting eighteen tons
of tires (above). In New York, volunteers
(below right) made door-to-door collections.
To conserve rubber, the landing wheels of
airplanes were sometimes replaced with
wooden discs (below left).

The housing shortage was so severe (left) that some people had to resort to living on houseboats (above).

The most severe shortage on the home front was that of adequate housing. About twenty million Americans relocated during the war. The population of Mobile, Alabama, a booming shipyard city, jumped 60 percent in just three years. Few new houses were built in industrial centers. The construction industry was working full time to put up factory complexes. Families moving to new cities slept in cars, garages, or woodsheds until they found housing. Single workers rented "hot beds" in private houses. The beds, which were rented for twenty-five cents for eight hours, often changed occupants with the shift changes at the local factory.

Home-front Americans delighted in one story that illustrated how critical the housing shortage had become. A Los Angeles newspaper reporter who was desperately looking for an apartment was sent one day to cover the shooting of a local gangster. He arrived at the scene, spoke to a police sergeant, confirmed that the gangster was dead, and scribbled the man's home address on a piece of paper. Then the reporter dashed off to the dead man's apartment building. "Your tenant is dead," he panted to the landlady. "Now, can I rent his apartment?" The woman shook her head, pointed, and said, "Sorry, but I just rented it to that police sergeant there."

The housing shortage contributed to one of the most tragic episodes of the home-front era. To answer the call for workers, more than a million southern blacks migrated to northern cities. Some sixty thousand blacks moved to Detroit, only to discover that many factories refused to hire them for jobs other than that of janitor. Worse yet, Detroit blacks were forced to live in a tiny, overcrowded slum called, ironically, Paradise Valley.

In June of 1943, thirty-five people were killed and hundreds more were injured when racial tensions in Detroit exploded into a terrible riot.

On one sultry June night in 1943, a fistfight between a white man and a black man broke out in Belle Island Park. Others joined in, and the fighting spilled into the streets, gathering fury as it spread. Federal troops had to be called in. When peace was finally restored thirty-six hours later, twenty-five blacks and nine whites were dead, and more than seven hundred people were injured. It was the worst incident of racial violence in the United States in twenty-five years.

Slowly, employment opportunities for blacks increased. Largely out of necessity, companies began hiring blacks for jobs from which they previously had been excluded. Sometimes the social change was painful. White transit workers in Philadelphia went on strike after the city hired eight black motormen to drive streetcars. The strike ended only after President Roosevelt sent armed troops to ride the streetcars with the black drivers. When the strike was over, the black drivers kept their jobs. Although black workers continued to earn substantially lower wages than whites, they began entering previously all-white trades and trade unions. For both women and blacks, the war years marked a critical period in the struggle for equality.

In June of 1944, General Dwight D. Eisenhower announced that Allied troops had stormed the beaches in northern France, thereby beginning the long-awaited invasion of Nazi-occupied Europe. Even though this meant that the war might soon be over, American civilians greeted the news of the invasion with anxiety as well as relief.

Everyone on the home front, including this wounded soldier recovering in a Chicago hospital, welcomed the news that the long-awaited Allied invasion of Nazi-occupied Europe had finally begun.

Overseas casualties were mounting at an appalling rate. American losses in the final twelve months of the war exceeded those of the first three-and-a-half years combined. Some fifteen hundred Marines died on the first day of the assault on Iwo Jima.

One night in October 1944, a strange event occurred in the household of young Rick Rosmarin in New York City. For no apparent reason, the bar-mitzvah picture of Stanley Rosmarin fell off the wall and crashed to the floor. The very next day a man knocked on the door and solemnly delivered a telegram from the War Department: "REGRET TO INFORM YOU YOUR SON STANLEY ROSMARIN WAS KILLED IN ACTION. . . ."

President Roosevelt, who had led the country for twelve difficult years, died just four months before the war ended.

Early 1945 saw Allied army troops streaking toward Germany while naval and marine forces edged closer to Japan. In April, Americans mourned the death of President Franklin Delano Roosevelt, who had led the country for twelve difficult years. On assuming office, the new president, Harry Truman, learned that Allied scientists were building an atomic bomb of enormous explosive power. The project to develop the bomb was so secret that Truman had not even known of its existence when he was vice-president.

Reporters listen attentively as President Truman reads the Japanese note of surrender.

Within a period of four months, Berlin fell, Adolf Hitler committed suicide, and Germany surrendered. Atomic bombs launched by the United States obliterated Hiroshima and Nagasaki, and Japan surrendered in September 1945. The war was over, but the world had entered a frightening atomic age.

Still, the people on the American home front rejoiced. Some went to church; others joined impromptu parades. No longer did families have to worry about that dreaded knock on the door. The cursed shortages would soon be over.

Like Americans everywhere, New Yorkers (above) and Chicagoans (opposite page) poured into the streets to celebrate the news that the war was finally over.

Thousands of New Yorkers packed Times Square to celebrate. Total strangers hugged and kissed one another and danced in the streets. In Chicago, children formed makeshift ranks and paraded down the avenues pounding sticks on garbage-can covers. All over the country, people sang and shouted, "It's over! The war's finally over!"

Above all, Americans celebrated the belief that lasting peace had come to the world. Never again, they hoped and prayed, would war rule their lives.

Newspaper accounts kept home-front Americans aware of what was happening overseas. These newspaper headlines tell the story of the war from beginning to end.

# Index

*About the Author*

Mr. Stein was born and grew up in Chicago. At eighteen he enlisted in the Marine Corps where he served three years. He was a sergeant at discharge. He later received a B.A. in history from the University of Illinois and an M.F.A. from the University of Guanajuato in Mexico.

Although he served in the Marines, Mr. Stein believes that wars are a dreadful waste of human life. He agrees with a statement once uttered by Benjamin Franklin: "There never was a good war or a bad peace." But wars are all too much a part of human history. Mr. Stein hopes that some day there will be no more wars to write about.